CLASSROOM
BULLETIN
BOARDS

Including:
Transparency
Patterns
and
3-D
Suggestions

With Learning Activities for Elementary Children

by Teresa Jones

STANDARD
PUBLISHING
Cincinnati, Ohio

Illustrated by Dan Grossman
Edited by Karen Brewer

The Standard Publishing Company, Cincinnati, Ohio
A division of Standex International Corporation
© 1994 by The Standard Publishing Company
All rights reserved
Printed in the United States of America

01 00 99 98 97 96 95 94   5 4 3 2 1

Library of Congress Cataloging-in-Publication Data

Jones, Teresa.
    Classroom bulletin boards : with learning activities for
elementary children / by Teresa Jones.
        p.   cm.
    ISBN 0-7847-0223-3
    1. Christian education--Bulletin boards.   2. Christian education
of children.   I. Title.
BV1535.25.J66   1994
268'.432--dc20   94-12870
                                CIP

Contents

Introduction

Bulletin boards are used in many different ways—to teach, to inform, and to extend lessons. Bulletin boards should be simple, easy to understand, and inviting. A bulletin board may be a part of a room divider, mounted on the wall, or cardboard covered with Con-Tact paper. Each bulletin board is composed of the background, message, and border.

Backgrounds may be colored paper, fabric, tissue paper, wallpaper, newspaper, burlap, or whatever adds variety and texture.

Lettering should be uniform in shape, size, and thickness. The letters can be mounted flat, or raised for a 3-D effect. Make your own letters by using stencils to trace on to paper or cloth. Letters can also be purchased. Choose a style that is easy to read. Add variety to your boards by overlapping letters, staggering them, or by adding your own touches such as putting dots or arrows at the tip of each letter. Laminating letters and figures used on your boards will make them look professional and will also help them last longer. Outline figures and letters to help them stand out from other parts of the bulletin board.

Use **borders** to cover rough edges and to frame your picture. Borders may be strips of colored paper, scalloped edging purchased at school or church supply stores, cut out shapes to compliment the message, or three-dimensional figures to grab the viewer's attention.

This book offers you a variety of ideas and challenges to create bulletin boards for your classroom. Crafts and activities extending the theme of the boards are also included to involve students in every sense.

Activities are not restricted to any one age level. They are labeled by level of difficulty for ease in selecting appropriately.

Easy   Intermediate   Difficult

How to Use the Transparency Patterns

It's Easy!

(**1**)   Remove the two transparencies from the book.

(**2**)   Select a pattern.

(**3**)   The best part is that with a transparency, any size object can be made. If you have a small bulletin board, make the object small. If you have a large board, make the object large. The transparency can also be reversed to change the direction and look of objects.

(**4**)   Cover the bulletin board and trace objects directly onto the background, or trace objects onto mounted paper. Then remove and cut out.

(**5**)   Add color as desired. Be creative! Use markers, crayons, paints, colored pencils, and fabric. Add a little color or a lot.

(**6**)   Save your creations and use them again and again!

God Saw That It Was Good

God looked at everything he had made, and it was very good. Genesis 1:31 (ICB)

Materials:

Transparency Patterns:	boy, girl, rabbit, deer
Background:	green and light blue paper, green marker
Border:	black scalloped
Lettering:	black
Stream:	blue paper, blue marker
Sun:	yellow paper, orange marker
Tree:	brown and green paper
Children:	white paper, assorted markers, fabric
Rabbits:	white paper, cotton balls
Deer:	brown paper

Directions: Cover the top one half of the board with light blue paper. Mount green paper along the bottom half of the board. Trim the top of the green paper into a "hilly" edge. Use a marker to draw in hills.

Cut a stream by freehand. Add ripple lines with a marker and mount to the board. Cut a tree trunk by freehand from brown paper. Use strips of green paper to make the tree top. Roll one end of the paper strips to make curls. Starting at the tree trunk, attach rows of curled paper strips for a 3-D effect.

Trace and cut out as many rabbits as desired. (Reverse the transparency and reduce or enlarge rabbits for variety.) Add cotton tails. Trace and cut out deer in the same way.

Trace and cut out children. Add color as desired using markers and fabric. Mount children and animals. Cut out a sun by freehand and outline with an orange marker. Mount the sun and letters. Finish the board with a scalloped border.

Favorite Animals

Materials:
copies of *National Geographic, Zoobooks, Ranger Rick,* or other magazines and
    calendars with animal pictures
poster board
black marker

Write "Our Favorite Animals That God Made" at the top of the poster board. Hang
the poster and ask students to search for pictures of their favorite animals. As students
attach their pictures to the poster, ask each student to tell why the animal is a favorite
and say, "I thank God for making a _____."

Animal Classification

Materials:
several large envelopes for each group of students
variety of animal pictures

Discuss animal classifications such as animals that are pets, animals found in the
Bible, and animals that climb trees. Allow students to suggest classifications.

Then divide students into small groups. Explain that each group will be given a
number of animal pictures to sort. Pictures are to be separated into envelopes according
to the classifications decided on by the large group. Allow students a set time to sort
their pictures. At the end of the time, discuss the variations in God's creation. Also talk
about how God made provisions for protecting animals such as coloring, climate, and
habitat.

Music

Sing to the tune of "Old MacDonald Had a Farm:"

    God created many kinds, E-I-E-I-O.
    And in the garden he made a duck, E-I-E-I-O.
    With a quack-quack here;
    And a quack-quack there;
    Here a quack; there a quack; everywhere a quack-quack!
    God created many kinds, E-I-E-I-O.

Continue singing verses substituting other animals and the sounds they make (i.e.
pig, lion, horse, chicken, cow, sheep, goat, dog).

God Keeps His Promise

This is the Lord's sign to you that the Lord will do what he has promised.
Isaiah 38:7 (NIV)

Materials:

Transparency Patterns:	rainbow with clouds and sun, ark, Noah and wife, elephant, sheep
Background:	white paper
Border:	blue scalloped
Lettering:	black
Water:	blue paper
Grass:	green paper
Rainbow, Clouds, and Sun:	markers or tempera paint in red, orange, yellow, green, blue, indigo, violet (top to bottom order), tinsel
Ark:	brown paper, black marker
Noah and Wife:	white paper, assorted markers
Animals:	white paper, assorted markers or paint

Directions: Cover the board. Trace the rainbow, clouds, and sun directly onto the background. Color the rainbow in the color order above with markers or paint. Outline clouds with a blue marker and attach tinsel to look like rain. Color the sun. Add the caption across the rainbow.

Tear paper into "waves" and attach to the lower left edge of the board. Staple strips of fringed green paper to the lower right edge for grass. Trace and cut out the ark. Mount on the waves.

Trace and cut out Noah with his wife, two elephants, and two sheep. Add color as desired and mount all on the grass.

Diorama

Materials:
   shoe box
   blue paint or paper
   assorted paper
   assorted markers and crayons
   small stones and twigs
   white tissue paper

Cut a 1" square in one end of the shoe box which will be the front. Paint the inside of the box blue or cover it with blue paper. In the back of the box, glue a rainbow made from paper. Draw, color, and cut out Noah. Place Noah near the center. Glue a few small stones with twigs and fire made of paper in the center to represent the altar Noah built in thanking God. Include animals, the ark, and Noah's family if desired. Glue white tissue paper across the top of the shoe box. Peek at the diorama through the hole.

Experiment

Materials:
   clear plastic one-liter bottle
   mineral oil
   water
   red and blue food coloring

Fill the clear one-liter bottle half full with mineral oil. Fill the other half with water. Observe with the students that the mineral oil does not change when the water is added. It remains the same.

Add red food coloring. Notice what happens. The food coloring mixes with the water but not the mineral oil. It still stays the same.

Add blue food coloring. Shake it gently. Observe what happens. The blue coloring mixes with the water but not the mineral oil. (An interesting point is that when shaking the mixture, the red and blue will separate but mix again when allowed to sit calmly.) Even though you shake the bottle or roll it from side to side, the mineral oil still doesn't mix with the water. It does not change.

God does not change. We may be tempted in different ways. There may be things that shake us up, but we can put our trust in God for he does not change. He is the same yesterday, today, and forever.

Role Play

Read Genesis 6-9 for background and discuss the story of Noah and the flood with your students. Let students choose some scenes involving Noah's life before, during, and after the flood to act out for the rest of the class.

Praise Him!

Let every creature praise his holy name for ever and ever. Psalm 145:21 (NIV)

Materials:

Transparency Patterns:	monkey, boy, girl, safari hat, peeled banana
Background:	green and light blue paper
Border:	yellow scalloped
Tree:	green, brown paper
Monkey:	brown and white paper, yellow marker
Boy and Girl:	white paper, assorted markers and fabric
Safari Hats:	brown paper
Peeled Bananas:	white paper, yellow marker
Unpeeled Bananas:	made by students in the activity

Directions: Cover the bottom third of the board with green paper and the top two-thirds with blue paper. Attach the border around its edge. Cut out a tree trunk by freehand from brown paper and mount to the left side of the board. Cut out large oval-shaped leaves by freehand from green paper. Fold in half lengthwise. Attach one end of the leaves near the top of the trunk. Bow out leaves for a 3-D effect.

Trace and cut out the monkey from brown paper. Trace and cut out his banana from white paper. Color the peel with a marker and glue on. Mount the monkey in the tree top.

Trace and cut out the boy and girl. Add color with markers and fabric as desired. Trace and cut out two safari hats. Slit on the broken lines and slip onto the children's heads. Trace and cut out a peeled banana. Color the peel with a marker. Mount the children with their hats and banana on the right side of the board.

Add the caption and randomly mount bananas made by students in the activity.

Praise His Name!

Materials:
  banana pattern, page 63
  yellow paper

Photocopy several bananas from page 63. Give each student a banana to cut out. Read Psalm 145:21. Ask students to write something to praise God for on their bananas. Add the bananas to the bulletin board.

An "A-peel" to Learn God's Word

Materials:
  banana pattern, page 63
  yellow paper

Photocopy and cut out several bananas from page 63. Write Psalm 145:21, putting each word on a separate paper banana. Read the verse together three times. Scramble the bananas with the words from the first sentence. Let the students put them in order. Read the verse together three times again. Scramble the second sentence. Let students put them in order.

Read the verse together three times. Choose a student to take a word out. Read the verse together with the students supplying the missing word. Continue to let students remove words for several rounds. In the end, each student should be able to say the verse on his own. When a student has memorized the verse, let that student write his/her name on a banana and add it to the bulletin board.

Tasting Party

Materials:

paper or poster board	banana chips (dehydrated banana slices)
black marker	peanut butter and mashed bananas mixed to make a spread
banana slices	banana jelly beans
	napkins, spoons, and small paper plates

Make a chart for students (separately or as a group) to fill out with these headings across the top: Looks Like, Tastes Like, Feels Like, Smells Like, Sounds Like. Leave space along the left side of the chart to name different banana items such as banana slices, banana chips, peanut butter and banana spread, and banana jelly beans. Fill the chart out for one item at a time. For example, give each student a banana slice. First, look at it. Write a describing word under Looks Like in the box across from Banana Slices. Continue to fill out the chart for each category and for each food item. Talk about how God has made us with many wonderful abilities. Among them are the abilities to look, taste, feel, smell, and hear.

Sing Praises

I will praise you, Lord, with all my heart.
I will tell all the miracles you have done.
I will be happy because of you.
God Most High, I will sing praises to your name.
Psalm 9:1, 2 (ICB)

Materials:

Transparency Pattern:	heart, music notes
Background:	red or pink wrapping paper with a small print
Border:	musical note pattern on page 62, black paper
Lettering:	white vinyl stick-on letters
Large Heart:	red paper, lace
Small Hearts:	pink paper, black marker
Musical Notes:	black paper

Directions: Cover the board. Trace and cut out a large red heart and attach lettering. Glue lace around its edge. Mount in the center of the board.

Add a musical note border across the top and bottom. Use the pattern on page 62 to fan-fold 3 1/8" high strips of paper into 5 3/4" wide rectangles. Place the note pattern on top of the folded paper, making sure broken lines of the pattern touch folded paper edges. Cut out the notes and unfold.

Trace and cut out small hearts. Write a student's name on each heart. Attach to the board around the large heart. Also add hearts made by students in the activities.

Trace and cut out musical notes to scatter randomly on the board.

Praise God for Friends

Materials:

pink, red, white paper heart transparency pattern (optional)
black marker cup

Make a supply of small red and pink hearts which say, "You're special because
_____." (Enlarge and photocopy the heart pattern on the transparency if desired.)
Ask each student to write something positive about each other student in the class on a
separate heart. Make a large white heart out of white paper for each student.

Begin by putting each student's name in a cup and drawing one out. Ask every other
student to read what he/she has written about the student whose name was drawn.
Attach all of the small hearts written about that student to a large white heart. Give the
large heart to the student to take home and share with parents. Allow time for each
student to be affirmed by classmates.

Making Conversation

Materials:

candy "conversation" hearts or red and pink paper hearts

Buy a bag of candy "conversation" hearts or make several "talking" paper hearts with
words or phrases written on them (i.e., You're cool!, I Luv U, Neat-O, PTL, 2 God B the
Glory!). Allow time for students to write a story using the hearts. Glue in a heart in
place of writing out those words in the story. You may want to write a few sentences as
an example. For instance,

Once I came home from school and found a (Surprise!) My dad had brought home a

puppy. I said "(Wow!) Thanks, dad. You are a (Cool Dude)." The puppy was (Great!) I

was very thankful for my dad's (Love).

Hearts of Praise

Materials:

pink paper
black marker
heart transparency pattern (optional)

Write verses of praise on several paper hearts. (Enlarge and photocopy the heart
pattern on the transparency if desired.) Some references may include: Psalm 7:17; 34:1-3;
35:28; 51:15; 66:1,2; 66:8; 71:8; 79:13; 92:1; 100:1-5; 106:48; 107:8. (Challenge older students
to find their own praise verses to write on the hearts.) Ask students to read the verses
on the hearts. Then allow students to write, "I praise God for _____" on each heart.
Add the hearts with verses and the hearts of praise to the bulletin board.

Jesus Calms the Storm

Jesus stood up and commanded the wind and the waves to stop. He said, "Quiet!
Be still!" Then the wind stopped, and the lake became calm. Mark 4:39 (ICB)

Materials:

Transparency Pattern:	Jesus in a boat
Background:	light blue paper or fabric
Border:	white scalloped
Lettering:	black
Water:	clear cellophane, aluminum foil, blue crepe paper
Jesus in a Boat:	white paper, assorted markers and paint
Conversation Balloon:	white paper

Directions: Cover the board. Cover the bottom third of the board with clear cellophane, making the
top edge "wavy." Line the top wavy edge with twisted aluminum foil. Use crepe paper to line a lower
row of waves. Attach the border around the edge of the board.

Trace and cut out Jesus and the boat. Add color as desired with markers and paint. Write "Mark 4:35-
41" on the boat. Cut out a conversation balloon by freehand. Add letters to the balloon and mount.

Mural

Materials:
   white paper or newsprint
   assorted watercolors, markers, and crayons

Using the seven verses of Mark 4:35-41 as separate scenes, make a mural telling the story of Jesus calming the sea. Divide a large strip of paper into seven sections. Let the students draw a scene for each verse and color the scenes with paint, markers, and crayons. When the mural is complete, students can take turns retelling the story.

A-B-C's

Materials:
   alphabet cereal or macaroni
   assorted crayons and markers
   file folder for each student

On a file folder turned sideways, have each student draw a picture of Jesus calming the sea. Then open the folders and instruct students to arrange cereal or macaroni letters to make words of a key verse such as Mark 4:41, "The followers were very afraid and asked each other, 'What kind of man is this? Even the wind and the waves obey him!'" (ICB). Instruct students to glue the words inside their folders. Students can share their pictures and retell the story. Opening the folder, they may read the verse to remind them of Jesus' power.

Music

Sing to the tune of "Mary Had a Little Lamb:"

   Jesus is the Son of God,
   Son of God,
   Son of God.
   Jesus is the Son of God;
   So, we worship Him.

   Jesus calmed the stormy sea,
   Stormy sea,
   Stormy sea.
   Jesus calmed the stormy sea;
   So, we worship Him.

Encourage the class to make up verses to continue the song (i.e., Jesus gives us love to share, Jesus prepares a place for us).

The Big Catch

Early the next morning Jesus stood on the shore. But the followers did not know that it was Jesus. Then he said to them, "Friends, have you caught any fish?" They answered, "No." He said, "Throw your net into the water on the right side of the boat, and you will find some." So they did this. They caught so many fish that they could not pull the net back into the boat. The follower whom Jesus loved said to Peter, "It is the Lord!" John 21:4-7 (ICB)

Materials:

Transparency Patterns:	fishermen
Background:	white and light blue paper
Border:	medium blue paper, chenille wires
Lettering:	red
Water:	clear cellophane
Fishermen:	white paper, assorted markers
Net:	fishnet (available in party supply stores)
Fish:	fish made by students in the activity

Directions: Cover the board with white paper on the top third and blue on the bottom two-thirds of the board. Make a scalloped edge where the two colors meet. Cover the blue paper (water) with clear cellophane for a "wet" look.

Attach a 3" wide strip of blue paper around the edge of the board. Form fish shapes with chenille wires, and glue to the border strip.

Trace and cut out two fishing boats with fishermen. (Reverse the transparency to make the two different.) Add color as desired. Mount boats at the top of the water.

Drape the net between the two boats. Attach the fish that students made in the activity so they are "caught" in the net. Mount lettering around the bottom edge of the net.

Stuffed Fish

Materials:
  fish pattern
  white paper
  paint, crayons, or markers
  newspaper or plastic bags
  stapler

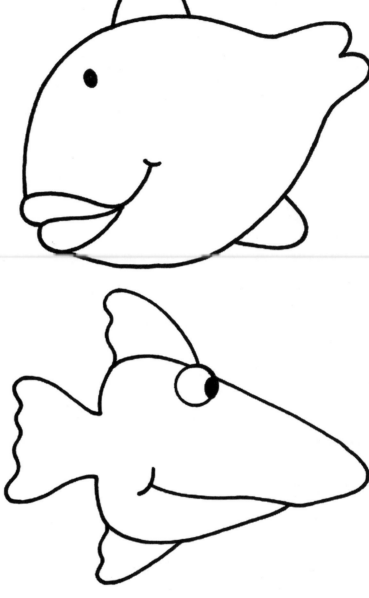

Photocopy the fish. (Enlarge to an appropriate size for the board.) Cut out the fish. Trace the fish and cut out an identical size plain fish. Using paint, markers or crayons, make designs on the fish. Talk about patterns and designs in things God made. Glue the edges of the two fish together except for the mouth. Stuff with crumpled newspaper or plastic bags. Staple the mouth shut. Put the fish in the net on the bulletin board or hang in the classroom.

"Let's Go Fishing!"

Materials:
  fish pattern
  wood dowel
  string
  magnet
  assorted paper
  paper clips

Make a fishing rod by tying string onto a wood dowel. Tie a magnet to the free end of the string. Copy and cut out a number of fish onto assorted colors of paper. Enlarge if desired. Write each word of a verse, such as "Come, follow me," Jesus said, "and I will make you fishers of men" (Matthew 4:19, NIV), on a separate fish. Slide a paper clip onto each fish.

Allow students to take turns "fishing." After the fish are caught, let students put the verse in order.

Hint: Make two fishing poles and two sets of fish to facilitate more participation and teamwork.

Look Straight Ahead

Keep your eyes focused on what is right.
Keep looking straight ahead to what is good. Proverbs 4:25 (ICB)

Materials:

Transparency Pattern:	cross and path
Background:	yellow and green paper
Border:	orange and brown paper
	footprints made by students
Lettering:	green
Cross and Path:	tan paper
Light Rays:	orange marker

Directions: Cover the board with yellow paper on the top third and green paper on the bottom two-thirds of the board.

Trace and cut out the cross and path. Mount in the center of the board. Use a marker to draw in light rays from the cross to the edge of the yellow paper. Mount the caption in the path.

Attach 3" wide strips of orange paper around the edge of the board. Ask students to trace their footprints onto brown paper, cut them out, and mount them on the orange border strip.

Rebus

Materials:
Bible
paper
pencils

Read Proverbs 4:20-26. Ask students to write the passage drawing objects or symbols to represent words where possible. For example:

Guard your 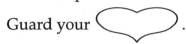 .

Have students exchange Scriptures and read the rebus created by a friend.

Look to Jesus

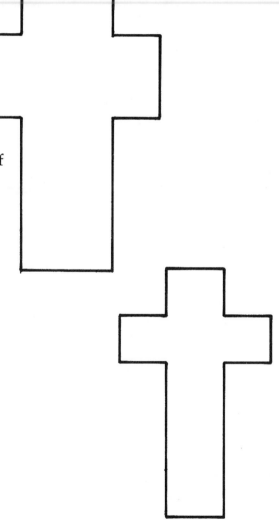

Materials:
cross patterns
newspaper
yellow tempera paint
fine point black permanent marker
clear nail polish
safety pin

Using the cross patterns here, trace each one out of newspaper six times. Cut them out, and glue the six large crosses together on top of each other. Glue the small crosses together in the same way. Glue the small crosses onto the large crosses; let them dry.

Paint the cross. When it is dry, use the marker to write "Look to Jesus" on the top cross. Coat the pin with clear nail polish and allow it to dry. Attach the safety pin to the back of the cross pin with glue.

Music

Sing to the tune of "Are You Sleeping?"

Are you walking? Are you walking?
On God's road? On God's road?
Jesus' path we'll follow;
Jesus' path we'll follow;
Eyes ahead; eyes ahead.

God's People—Caring and Sharing

To this you were called, because Christ suffered for you, leaving you an example, that you should follow in his steps. 1 Peter 2:21 (NIV)

Materials:

Background:	tan paper
Border:	fall colored silk leaves
Lettering:	orange
Tree:	brown paper, leaves made by students in the activity

Directions: Cover the board. Add silk leaves in the corners as a border.

Cut out a trunk by freehand. Mount in the center of the board. Use leaves that students made in the activity to overlap as the tree top.

Add lettering.

Colorful Leaves

Materials:
  assorted fall colors of paper
  black markers

Let students select sheets of paper to trace their hands and cut them out. Ask each student to write words describing God's people as helpers (i.e., helping, caring, sharing, doers) on their paper hands. Or ask students to write something they do as helpers (i.e., clean their room, take out trash, obey). Attach the hands to the bulletin board tree for its leaves.

Each Helper Is Special

Materials:
  ink pad
  damp cloth or moist towelettes

Talk about how each person is special to God. He created us uniquely. We each have our own fingerprints, our own voices, and our own abilities. Since each person has different abilities, each person may be able to help in different ways. This is good because people need many different kinds of help.
  Let students put their fingerprints with signatures on the bulletin board tree trunk.

Helping Hands

Materials:
  chalk
  chalkboard

Write phrases and verses using the words "hand" or "hands" on slips of paper. One person will pick a slip of paper that has a phrase or verse written on it. Without using words, that person will draw pictures on a chalkboard to get the class to guess the phrase or verse. Some suggestions to use may include the following:
  I can't think of anything right off *hand*.
  They won *hands* down.
  "My time is at *hand*" (Matthew 26:18, KJV).
  "Like clay in the *hand* of the potter" (Jeremiah 18:6, NIV).
  "In the hollow of his *hand*" (Isaiah 40:12, NIV).
  "At the right hand of God" (Mark 16:19, NIV).
  Give me a *hand*.
  I've got to *hand* it to you.
  "Father, into your *hands* I commit my spirit" (Luke 23:46, NIV).

Aim to Be A Good Friend

Jonathan felt very close to David.
He loved David as much as he loved himself. 1 Samuel 18:1 (ICB)

Materials:

Transparency Patterns:	archer, target, arrow, "Aim to Be A Good Friend"
Background:	red paper
Border:	medium blue paper
Lettering:	black marker or black letters
Archer:	white paper, assorted markers
Target:	white paper, assorted markers
Arrows:	medium blue paper, black marker

Directions: Cover the board. Trace and cut out several arrows, and mount around the board's edge to make a border. Trace and cut out the archer. Add color as desired. Instead of tracing the hat feather, attach a real feather. Mount in the bottom right corner.

Trace and cut out the target. Color each circle in the target a different color as desired. Mount in the upper left corner. Trace and cut out four additional arrows. Write on each arrow as illustrated with a marker, and mount arrows in word order. Trace the caption from the transparency directly onto the background with a marker or attach any plain black letters to the board.

Variations:

1. "Aim for Godly Characteristics" (Ephesians 4:32)—Write words such as kindness, compassionate, and forgiving on the arrows.
2. "Aim for the Best"—Write students' names on the arrows. Put stickers on the arrows for attendance, bringing Bibles, memorizing Scripture, and bringing friends.

Friendship Poem

Materials:

    heavy, 5" paper plate
    shell-shaped macaroni
    gold spray paint
    copies of the Friendship Poem below
    ribbon

Glue macaroni around the edges of the paper plate to make a frame. Spray the frame with gold paint. Cut out the Friendship Poem and glue it to the center of the frame. Glue a loop of ribbon to the back of the plate to form a hanger. Give this as a gift to a good friend, or keep it to hang as a reminder to be a good friend like David and Jonathan were to each other.

Friendship Poem
by Teresa Jones

What kind of friend are you to me?
What kind of friend am I to you?
The kind Jesus would want us to be;
The kind who shows love in all that we do;
The kind who is giving and willing to share;
The kind who will listen and always be there;
The kind who is loving no matter what;
The kind who forgives and remembers not.
Jesus is a friend to you and me.
He is God's Son and always will be.

Friendship Gift

Materials:

    four frozen juice can lids
    paint that will adhere to metal
    alphabet macaroni
    red, blue, and purple markers
    wide ribbon
    narrow ribbon

Rhyme:

    Roses are red;
    Violets are blue;
    Friends are special,
    Thank God for you!

Paint the juice lids. Sort alphabet macaroni to spell out the rhyme. Glue a line of the rhyme onto each lid. Color the word "red" with a red marker. Color the word "blue" with a blue marker. Color "Thank God for you!" with a purple marker.

Cut a piece of wide ribbon long enough to space out the four lids in a row plus three inches. Fold the top back to form a casing. Lay a length of narrow ribbon across the wide ribbon before gluing the fold down. Tie the narrow ribbon to form a hanger. Position the lids in order on the front of the vertical piece of ribbon. Glue them in place.

This Is My Son

Jesus took Peter, James, and John the brother of James up on a high mountain. They were all alone there. While Peter was talking, a bright cloud covered them. A voice came from the cloud. The voice said, "This is my Son and I love him. I am very pleased with him. Obey him!" Matthew 17:1, 5 (ICB)

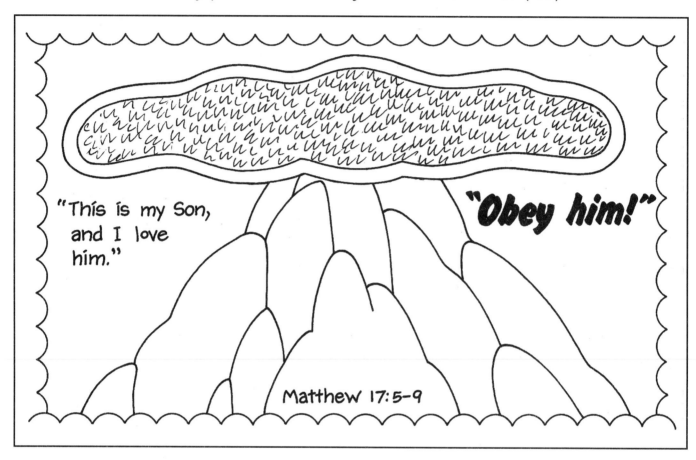

Materials:

Transparency Pattern:	mountain
Background:	blue paper
Border:	black scalloped
Lettering:	black letters or black marker
Mountain:	gray paper, black marker
Cloud:	white paper, white facial tissue, gold foil paper, blender

Directions: Cover the board. Trace and cut out the mountain and add details with a marker. Attach the mountain at the bottom of the board. Add the scalloped border to the board's edge.

Cut out two clouds by freehand—a large cloud from gold foil paper and a slightly smaller cloud from white paper.

Drop a facial tissue into a blender. Cover and turn on high speed for five seconds. Glue the shredded tissue to the white cloud. Shred additional tissues as needed.

Mount the gold cloud over the mountain top. Mount the white cloud on top of the gold cloud.

Write the Scripture reference onto the mountain with a marker. Write the scripture directly onto the background with a marker or attach letters.

Mountain Collage

Material:
   paper
   mountain transparency pattern (optional)
   old Sunday school visuals, VBS visuals, and church bulletins

Divide students into small groups. Provide a large sheet of paper with a mountain outline on it for each small group. (Draw by freehand or use the transparency pattern.) Let the students select and cut out pictures from the life of Christ to cover the mountain. Students may want to lay the pictures down on the paper to arrange and rearrange before they glue them. Hang completed collages around the room. Allow time for students to share their collages and to tell what they know about specific scenes which are shown.

Small Class Option: Work as one group to cover the mountain on the bulletin board.

Heavenly Dove

Materials:
   9" white paper plate
   dove pattern, page 63
   crayons and markers
   glitter
   yarn
   hole punch

In Matthew 3:17 a voice from heaven said, "This is my Son and I love him. I am very pleased with him" (ICB). Then the Spirit of God descended like a dove and lit on Jesus.
   Make a dove from the paper plate as a reminder of God's affirmation. Begin by folding the paper plate in half, top in. Glue the halves together around the edge. Using the pattern on page 63, cut out pieces of the paper plate to form the dove silhouette. Write, "Jesus is God's Son" along the bottom edge. Draw an eye on the head. Let students decorate the dove using crayons, markers, and glitter. Punch a hole near the middle of the top. Tie a length of yarn through the hole. Hang doves in the classroom to "fly" as reminders of the Spirit's message.

Names for Jesus

Materials:
   colored chalk

The Bible has many names for God's Son, Jesus (i.e., Immanuel, bread of life, Prince of Peace). Take students outdoors and fill the sidewalk with as many names for Jesus as they can think of. Write with colored chalk that rain will wash away.

A Special Birth Is Announced

The angel said to her, "Don't be afraid, Mary, because God is pleased with you. Listen! You will become pregnant. You will give birth to a son, and you will name him Jesus." Luke 1:30, 31 (ICB)

Materials:

Transparency Pattern:	Mary sitting on a rock, angel head and arms
Background:	light blue paper
Border:	garland
Lettering:	black
Mary:	white paper, gray tempera paint, sponge, assorted markers
Angel:	gold and silver foil wrapping paper, white paper, assorted markers

Directions: Cover the board and attach the garland around its edge. Trace and cut out Mary sitting on the rock. Sponge paint the rock to add texture. Add color to Mary with markers and fabric as desired. Mount Mary on the left side of the board.

Fan-fold a rectangle of silver foil wrapping paper into wings. Make the angel's gown by wrapping gold foil paper into a cone shape. Flatten slightly and trim bottom edge. Trace and cut out the angel's arms and head. Add color with markers as desired. Mount angel wings, topped with cone gown, and head and arms to complete the angel.

Add the caption.

Button Angel Ornament

Materials:
- angel pattern
- poster board
- yellow marker
- extra fine point, gold paint marker
- fine point black marker
- pink crayon
- gold cord trim or yarn
- assorted flat white buttons
- wax paper
- flat topped shank button
- 1/8" wide yellow or gold ribbon
- gold foil wire twist with stars or chenille wire
- Optional: hot glue gun

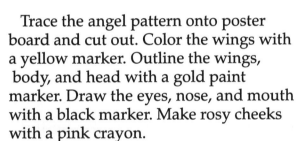

Trace the angel pattern onto poster board and cut out. Color the wings with a yellow marker. Outline the wings, body, and head with a gold paint marker. Draw the eyes, nose, and mouth with a black marker. Make rosy cheeks with a pink crayon.

Glue gold cord trim or yarn around the skirt outline. Starting at the bottom of the skirt and working up, cover with a thin layer of glue, and fill the area with an assortment of white buttons. Cover the angel with a piece of wax paper; place a book on top, and dry over night.

While the angel is drying, make the hanger and halo. Start with the shank button. Thread an 8" piece of ribbon through the button shank and tie a knot to form a loop for hanging the ornament. Cut a 6" piece of gold wire twist or chenille wire. Form a round halo approximately 1" in diameter and twist to hold the shape. Thread the remaining wire end through the shank in the button. Twist the wire around the shank and bend the circle at a 90° angle from the front of the button. Pull the ribbon loop through the halo. Glue the halo and ribbon into place on the back of the button. (White glue will take a long time to dry and will not be as secure as an adult gluing it with a hot glue gun.)

After the angel has dried well, glue the flat side of the button to the back of the head with the halo extending over the front of the angel. Dry for several hours.

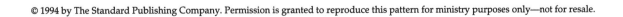

Jesus Is Born

While Joseph and Mary were in Bethlehem,
the time came for her to have the baby. She gave birth to her first son.
There were no rooms left in the inn. So she wrapped the baby with cloths
and laid him in a box where animals are fed. Luke 2:6, 7 (ICB)

Materials:

Transparency Patterns:	Mary, Joseph, manger, Jesus, sheep
Background:	light blue felt
Border:	cardboard, wood grain Con-Tact paper
Lettering:	black
Mary, Joseph, and Jesus:	white paper, assorted markers and fabric
Manger:	cardboard, wood grain Con-Tact paper
	raffia paper or straw
Sheep:	white paper, cotton

Directions: Cover the board. Cut cardboard into three inch wide strips and cover with the Con-Tact paper. Mount the strips around the edge of the board for a border.

Trace and cut out Mary, Joseph, and Jesus. Add color as desired with markers and fabric.

Trace and cut out the manger. Cover with wood grain Con-Tact paper. Mount the manger and add raffia paper or straw in and under the manger. Also mount Mary, Joseph, and Jesus.

Trace and cut out as many sheep as desired. (Reverse the transparency for sheep facing both directions.) Cover with cotton and add to the scene.

Mount the caption .

Christmas Wreath

Materials:
  manger scene from used Christmas greeting card
  green felt
  fabric glue
  jigsaw puzzle pieces
  green Fleck Stone spray paint
  newspaper
  red tissue paper
  green ribbon or yarn

Cut the manger scene into a circle. (Plastic lids make good circle patterns.) Cut a larger circle out of green felt. Glue the manger scene to the center of the felt circle.

Spray paint several jigsaw puzzle pieces. Let dry. Glue puzzle pieces around the edge of the circle onto the felt and overlapping the scene. Glue a second layer of puzzle pieces on top of the first layer. Position them to cover empty spaces. (Not every space will be covered. The pieces will resemble evergreen branches.)

Glue red tissue paper wads onto the puzzle pieces for berries. Glue a loop of ribbon or yarn to the back to hang the wreath.

Place Mats

Materials:
  4" red paper square
  4" white paper square
  12" x 18" green paper
  white paper
  crayons and markers
  clear Con-Tact paper (optional)

Fold the white and red squares in half. Holding the half-squares on the folded sides, cut out hearts. Begin at the bottom corner of the fold and cut half a heart shape. Open up the hearts. Glue the white heart on the left side of the green paper. Turn the red heart upside down. Put in on top of the white heart. The point of the red heart should touch the center of the dip of the white heart. Glue into place. Cut out a white circle approximately the size of a half dollar. Place it on the hearts so that the circle covers the point where the two hearts overlap and extends above the white heart. Glue in place to make a heart angel. Draw eyes and a mouth on the angel. Write "Glory to the new born King!" on the mat. Make enough for the whole family. To keep, cover with clear Con-Tact paper.

Optional: Use this as a project to brighten the mealtime of nursing home residents.

Guard My Mouth Lord

Set a guard over my mouth, O Lord;
keep watch over the door of my lips. Psalm 141:3 (NIV)

Materials:

Transparency Patterns:	girl, boy, zipped lips
Background:	pink paper
Border:	purple scalloped
Lettering:	purple
Lips:	neon pink paper, black permanent marker
	silver metallic paint
Girl and Boy:	white paper, assorted markers

Directions: Cover the board.

Trace and cut out the zipped lips. Trace the zipper with a black permanent marker. Paint inside the black lines with metallic paint. Mount in the center of the board.

Trace and cut out the girl and boy. Add color as desired. Mount at the bottom of the board, overlapping the lips.

Add the caption above the lips, and mount the border around the board's edge.

Tic-Tac-Cover

Materials:
  6" square of poster board
  black marker
  ruler
  10 2" squares of poster board
  standard size envelope
  10 stickers—five each of two styles
  3" x 5" card
  assorted sized buttons

Making the game: Begin with a 6" square of poster board. Divide the board into nine 2" squares by drawing two lines two inches apart both horizontally and vertically. Glue the envelope to the back of the board.

Place one sticker on each of the ten 2" square poster board pieces. Buzzy Bee stickers published by Standard Publishing are suggested. Five of the squares may say, "Be Polite!" The other five may say, "Be Thankful."

Playing the game: Divide students into pairs and give a game to each pair. Write a verse such as Psalm 141:3 on a 3" x 5" card. Ask each pair to read the verse aloud, together or one at a time. Next, divide the 2" cards so that one person will have the "Be Polite" cards and the other person will have the "Be Thankful" cards.

The two will take turns placing a card onto the game board. The one getting three cards in a row wins the game. The three may be in a row going across, up and down, or diagonally. The winner then covers a word in the verse with a button, and the loser must try to read the verse with the hidden word. Separate the cards and begin again. Play until all words in the verse are covered. When the play is finished, store the ten cards in the envelope.

Matching Lips

Materials:
  red paper
  assorted markers

Cut several 4" wide lips from red paper. Use the transparency pattern if desired.

Help students make a list of things or words that God would desire to be on our lips (i.e., compliments, prayer, "I'm sorry," "Would you like to come?").

Ask students to write each item on the list onto two paper lips. Play "concentration" by spreading out all lips face down. Take turns selecting two lips. If they match, remove them from play and select again until all pairs are found.

He Has Risen!

He is not here; he has risen, just as he said.
Come and see the place where he lay. Matthew 28:6 (NIV)

Materials:

Transparency Patterns:	Jesus and the tomb
Background:	black
Border:	yellow scalloped
Lettering:	white
Tomb:	gray paper, black marker
Light Splash:	yellow paper
Jesus:	white paper, assorted markers

Directions: Cover the board. Trace and cut out the tomb separately. Add details with a marker and color the entrance to the tomb black. Mount on the right side of the board. Attach the border around the edge of the board.

Trace and cut out the splash of light separately. Mount to the left of the tomb.

Trace and cut out Jesus. Add color as desired. Mount in the splash of light. Add the caption.

The Stone Rolled Away

Materials:
  6" and 5" gray paper square
  black marker
  8" square of yellow poster board
  paper fastener
  white chenille wire

Cut a large rock out of the 6" gray paper square to represent the tomb. Color a black opening on the front. Glue the tomb to the poster board. Cut a smaller rock out of the 5" gray square big enough to cover the black opening. Place the small rock on top of the opening and attach at the bottom with a paper fastener so that the stone can be rolled away. Form a stick figure out of the chenille wire. Glue it to the side of the tomb. Write the words, "He Arose!" at the top.

Double Concentration

Materials:
  24 3" x 5" cards
  poster board
  markers

Making the game: Write Matthew 28:6 on a sheet of poster board with a number above each word and the reference.

1 2 3   4   5 6   7   8 9 10 11   12

"He is not here; he has risen, just as he said" (Matthew 28:6, NIV).

Write the same words from the poster and the Bible reference on separate index cards. Write the numbers one through twelve on separate index cards, too. Shuffle the 24 word and number cards. Place them face down on the table. Write a letter on each card (word cards and number cards together) beginning with A.

Playing the game: Mix the cards and place them on the table with the letters showing. Instruct students to take turns choosing two letter cards, trying to match a number and a word card according to the poster. If no match is made, cards remain on the table, letter side up. If a match is made, cards are removed from play. After all pairs have been matched, put the cards in order and read the verse together.

Faith

Faith comes from hearing the Good News. Romans 10:17 (ICB)

Materials:

Transparency Pattern:	faith design
Background:	white paper
Boarder:	red scalloped
Faith Design:	black, yellow, and red markers, skin-tone colored pencil

Directions: Cover the board and mount the border around its edge. Trace the faith design directly onto the background. Color the ear skin-tone, the arrow yellow, and FAITH red.

Mobile

Materials:

yarn

plastic straw

letter stencils

assorted paper

assorted markers

faith design transparency pattern (optional)

Thread a 28" piece of yarn through the straw and tie it with a loop for hanging the mobile. Using letter stencils, trace and cut out the letters F-A-I-T-H. Glue the top of each letter onto the horizontal straw. Cut out an ear by freehand or use the transparency pattern. Write Romans 10:17 on it. Tie it to the straw with an 8" length of yarn between the letters F and A.

Cut out a Bible by freehand or use the transparency pattern. Tie it to the straw with an 8" length of yarn between the letters T and H.

Who Said It?

Materials:

letter-size manila folder

adhesive magnetic strip

8 3" x 5" cards

letter-size envelope

Making the game: Use six cards to cut six conversation balloons (see bulletin board illustration on page 14) by freehand. Cut remaining cards into 1" x 3" strips. Write a quote on each balloon card. Write the name of the person quoted on each strip card. Use the following verses or any from recent lessons.

1.	"Here am I. Send me!" (NIV).	Isaiah	Isaiah 6:8
2.	"You are looking for Jesus the Nazarene, who was crucified. He has risen! . . . Go, tell his disciples and Peter" (NIV).	Man in a white robe	Mark 16:6, 7
3.	"Praise be to the God of Shadrach, Meshach and Abednego, who has sent his angel and rescued his servants!" (NIV).	Nebuchadnezzar	Daniel 3:28
4.	"You will again see the distinction between the righteous and the wicked, between those who serve God and those who do not" (NIV).	the Lord Almighty	Malachi 3:18
5.	"Leave the sanctuary, for you have been unfaithful; and you will not be honored by the Lord God" (NIV).	Azariah to Uzziah	2 Chronicles 26:18
6.	"Faith comes from hearing the message, and the message is heard through the word of Christ" (NIV).	Paul	Romans 10:17

Adhere a piece of magnetic strip on the back of each balloon and each strip. Next, put pieces of magnetic strip inside of the folder, positioning them so that the balloon quotes will have the speakers below them. Keep the cards in an envelope taped to the back of the folder.

Playing the game: Match the quote and the speaker by placing the cards on the magnets. Provide the Scripture references for students to check their own work.

Help Others

*I was hungry and you gave me something to eat, I was thirsty and you
gave me something to drink, I was a stranger and you invited me in,
I needed clothes and you clothed me, I was sick and you looked after me,
I was in prison and you came to visit me.* Matthew 25:35, 36 (NIV)

Materials:

Transparency Pattern:	helping scenes
Background:	white paper
Border:	tan paper
Lettering:	black
Helping Scenes:	assorted markers

Directions: Cover the board. Ask students to trace their hands onto tan paper and cut them out to use
as a border. (Each student may need to make several.)

Trace the helping scenes directly onto the background. Let students add color as desired.

Helping Hands Coupons

Materials:

assorted paper   coupon pattern below

Make coupons redeemable upon request and mutual agreement of time. Coupons could be made to help at home, at church, or at the home of a shut-in, elderly person, or working mom. Lead students to identify needs that they can meet. Depending on the age and ability of the students, the coupons will vary in the service that can be supplied. Encourage each student to make at least five coupons stating what job they can do such as sweeping, sharpening pencils, raking leaves, reading to a young child, etc.

To make coupons, let students trace their hands onto paper and cut them out. Complete and glue a coupon to each hand. Photocopy the coupons below. Ask students to fill in the blanks and glue one to each hand. Staple five hands together to make a book or give them individually.

This coupon entitles _____	This coupon entitles _____
to _____.	to _____.
Serving Christ, _____	Serving Christ, _____

Let Your Light Shine!

Materials:

3" Styrofoam ball   black marker
knife   hole punch
roll of Life Savers   8" x 8" foil gift wrap
aluminum foil   glitter glue
yellow chenille wire   1/4" wide ribbon
stiff paper

In the Sermon on the Mount, Jesus taught his followers to be the light of the world. Make a candle as a reminder of Matthew 5:14-16.

Cut the Styrofoam ball in half. Place one piece of Styrofoam flat on the table. Hollow out a hole 1" in diameter and 3/4" deep in the center of the mound, big enough to stand the Life Savers snugly in place. Wrap the Life Saver roll in aluminum foil to make a candle. Insert the candle into the hole in the center of the mound. Form a flame with the yellow chenille wire. Bend the bottom of the flame and glue it to the top of the candle.

Write Matthew 5:16 on a small piece of stiff paper with a marker. Punch a hole in the paper. Place the Styrofoam in the center of the foil gift wrap. Cut a 10" piece of ribbon. String the memory verse onto the ribbon. Gather the foil paper over the Styrofoam and around the bottom of the candle. Tie it with the ribbon.

Using the glitter glue, put a little glitter along the top and sides of the candle to look like dripping wax.

Mold Me Lord

Like clay in the hand of the potter, so are you in my hand,
O house of Israel. Jeremiah 18:6 (NIV)

Materials:

Transparency Pattern:	potter
Background:	tan paper
Border:	brown scalloped
Lettering:	green
Potter:	white paper, assorted markers, gray tempera paint

Directions: Cover the board and attach the border around its edge. Trace and cut out the potter and potter's wheel. Finger paint the clay pot. Add the rest of the color as desired. Mount on the board and add clay splashes with finger paint directly on the background. Add the caption.

Clay Play

Here are two different recipes to make clay. Each will keep up to a year if kept in a plastic bag. Make colored clay by adding food coloring if desired.

Encourage students to be creative as they mold something out of the clay.

Materials:
1 cup flour
1 cup water
1 teaspoon cream of tartar
1/2 cup salt
1 Tablespoon oil

Put all of the ingredients in a pan and stir while cooking over medium heat. Cook until the mixture pulls from the side of the pan, forming a ball.

Materials:
2 cups salt
1 cup water
1 cup cornstarch

Mix 2 cups of salt and 2/3 cup water in pan. Heat 3-4 minutes, but do not boil. Mix cornstarch and 1/2 cup cold water together. Add to the heated mixture and stir. Continue heating until the mixture starts thickening and becomes the consistency of dough.

Pinch Pot

Materials:
clay
tempera paint
clear spray lacquer

Have students roll a small handful of clay into a ball. Work with the clay like a softball—back and forth in their hands. Insert their thumb into the middle of the clay and rotate the ball, pressing the thumb to the fingers against the clay to open the pot. Continue doing this until the desired shape of the pot is obtained. Use different tools (i.e., pencils, nail file) to create a textured surface. Let pots dry. Paint the pots with tempera or poster paint. Spray them with a clear lacquer to preserve the paint.

Discuss how the students were the ones to determine the shape of their pots. They started with shapeless clay and made it into something useful. God tells Jeremiah that Israel is like clay in his hands (Jeremiah 18). God is in control.

Dry Bones, Hear the Word of the Lord

This is how you, my people, will know that I am the Lord.
I will open your graves and cause you to come up from them.
And I will put my Spirit inside you. You will come to life. Ezekiel 37:14 (ICB)

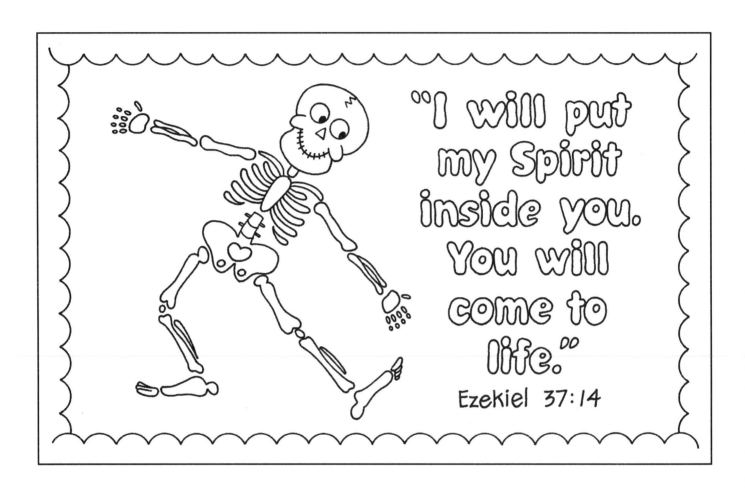

Materials:

Transparency Pattern:	skeleton
Background:	black paper
Border:	light blue scalloped
Lettering:	light blue
Skeleton:	white paper, black marker

Directions: Cover the board and attach the border around its edge. Trace the skeleton and cut out in one piece, although bones are disconnected. Mount the skeleton and Scripture with reference.

Pantomime

Write situations in which people have experienced new life through Jesus and the Holy Spirit onto slips of paper. Let students choose a situation and pantomime it for the class. Some situations may include:

I was blind, but now I see.
I was lame, but now I walk.
I was dead, but now I am alive.
I used to fight a lot, but now I am a peacemaker.

Story Writing

Guide students working alone or with a partner to write stories beginning with, "If I Were Ezekiel in the Valley of Dry Bones. . . ." Stories should describe the wondrous sight of seeing the bones rise up and come to life.

Ask these questions to help students get started: What kind of person was Ezekiel? How do you think he felt when he was told to prophesy to the dry bones?

Any Clues?

Materials:
crossword puzzle answer gird below
graph paper

Photocopy the crossword puzzle answer grid below for students. Using chapter 27 of Ezekiel, let students write clues for the answers to the puzzle. Draw a blank crossword puzzle on graph paper and give the graph paper and clues to another class to complete.

```
              L
          B O N E S
            R   Z
            D   E       V
                K       A
        S P I R I T     L
          R   E         L
          O     L I F E E
          P             Y
    B R E A T H
          E
          S
        D R Y
```

Examine Yourself

A man ought to examine himself before he eats of the bread and drinks of the cup.
1 Corinthians 11:28 (NIV)

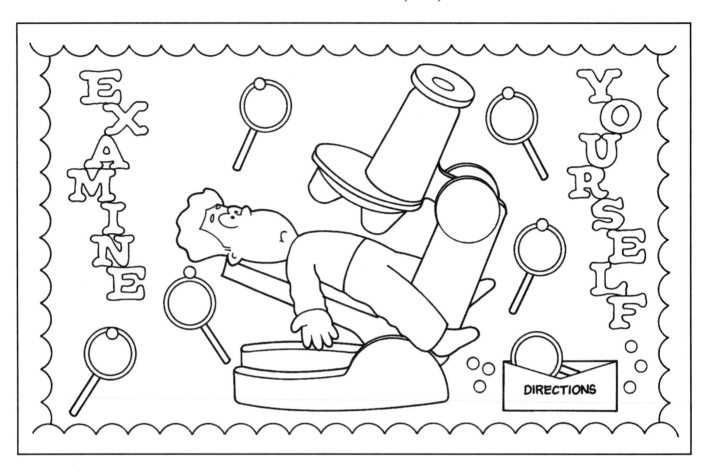

Materials:

Transparency Pattern:	microscope with boy
Background:	red paper
Border:	black scalloped
Lettering:	black
Microscope With Boy:	white paper, assorted markers
Magnifying Glasses:	several magnifying glasses photocopied from page 62
Directions:	large envelope, photocopied magnifying glasses
	thumb tacks

Directions: Cover the board and attach the border around its edge. Trace and cut out the microscope with the boy. Add color as desired and mount in the center of the board. Add the caption on each side.

Place a large envelop in the bottom right corner with the following directions:

Write a praise or poem on a magnifying glass to thank God for his grace.
Then add your magnifying glass to the board.

Cut out the photocopied magnifying glasses and insert them in the envelope. Place several thumb tacks nearby.

Silhouettes

Materials:
filmstrip projector
black paper
assorted paper

Make silhouettes of students by shining a filmstrip projector on each one and tracing the head outlines onto black paper. Cut each one out and mount on a sheet of colored paper. Have students fill out interview sheets to give word pictures of who they are. Then mount silhouettes and interview sheets around the room.

Sample interview statements may include the following:

Hello, my name is _____. My family consists of _____. We live in a/an _____. I have _____ pets. They are _____. When I am not at church or school, I like to _____. My favorite color is _____ because it reminds me of _____. My favorite Bible story is ____ _____. I am good at _____. If I had $10,000.00, I would _____.

Other options: Mix up interview sheets. Read or reveal parts of each and guess who wrote what. Instead of interview sheets, have students write short biographical sketches about themselves.

● ● ● ● ● ● ● ● ● ● ● ● ●
How Do You Rate?

Romans 12:9-19 admonishes us to live in harmony with one another. Read the list of attitudes and actions that are helpful for us to practice in our daily lives. Circle the number of the ones you already practice doing well. Choose one specific item to work on this week and decide how to accomplish it. Make a commitment and watch for opportunities to let the Lord work through you.

1. Love sincerely.
2. Hate what is evil; cling to what is good.
3. Be devoted to others in brotherly love.
4. Serve the Lord with spiritual fervor.
5. Be joyful in hope.
6. Be patient in affliction.
7. Be faithful in prayer.
8. Share with God's people in need.
9. Practice hospitality.
10. Bless those who persecute you.
11. Rejoice with those who rejoice.
12. Mourn with those who mourn.
13. Live in harmony with others.
14. Live at peace with everyone.
15. Overcome evil with good.

This week I will _____.

● ● ● ● ● ● ● ● ● ● ● ● ●

A Parable About Seed

The seed on good soil stands for those with a noble and good heart,
who hear the word, retain it, and by persevering produce a crop. Luke 8:15 (NIV)

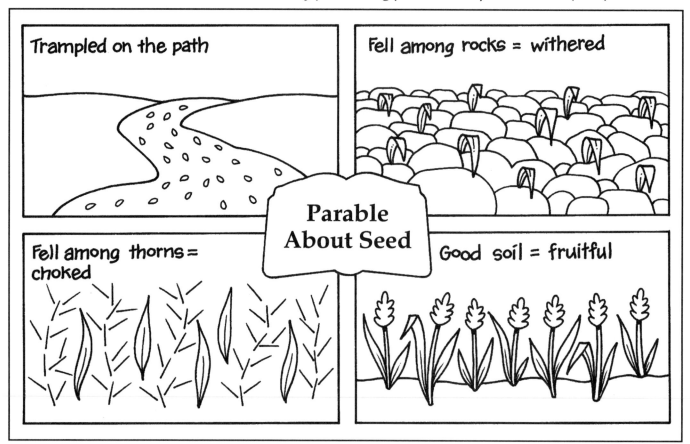

Materials:

Transparency Pattern:	fruitful plant, Bible outline
Background:	light blue paper
Border:	wide black ribbon
Lettering:	black marker, white paper, black letters
Trampled Seed Picture:	green and brown paper, popcorn
Withered Seed Picture:	gray and green paper, gray marker
Choked Seed Picture:	green paper, toothpicks
Fruitful Seed Picture:	green paper, green and beige felt

Directions: Cover the board. Use the ribbon to make a border and divide the board into four framed pictures.

Trampled Seed: Cover the bottom two-thirds of the picture with green paper. Cut a path by freehand from brown paper. Glue popcorn on the path. Mount after drying.

Withered Seed: Cut several rocks by freehand and outline with a marker. Mount overlapping rocks. Cut several thin strips of green paper for the withered plants. Place plants among the rocks and attach at the bottom only, allowing the strips to fall forward. (Curl strips around a pencil to help them droop.)

Choked Seed: Cut a few leaves by freehand. Place them randomly in the picture. Glue toothpicks onto the picture in an array to make a jumbled mass of thorns.

Fruitful Seed: Cover the bottom fourth of the picture with green paper. Trace the fruitful plant onto green felt and cut out. Trace the grain head onto beige felt. Cut out and glue onto the plant. Mount plants.

Write the description with a marker inside each picture. Trace and cut out the Bible outline and attach the caption. Mount the Bible in the center of the board.

Growing Plants

Materials:
    Styrofoam egg carton
    baby food jar
    water
    four paper towels
    seeds (i.e., beans, popcorn)

Talk to students about how important it is that plants be rooted firmly in order to grow. As Christians, we need to be firmly rooted in God's Word so that we can experience growth through him to become strong, healthy, and fruitful. To better understand plant growth, plant seeds and observe their growth.

Open up the egg carton. Break off the hump in the center of the lid. The lid will be the base for the planted seeds. Balance the carton on top of a baby food jar which is 3/4 full of water. Fold a paper towel in half lengthwise. Fold it in half again. Lay one end of the towel on the lid. The other end of the towel will go through the hole in the lid and into the jar below. Repeat this procedure with another paper towel so that the bottom of the lid is covered. This will serve as a "wick" to keep the towels moist. Fold another paper towel and place it over the two. Place twelve seeds on the top paper towel. Fold another paper towel to cover the seeds. Sprinkle some water on the top towel to dampen it. Close the carton and place where the seeds will be undisturbed.

Felt Banner

Materials:
    18" x 24" felt piece
    fabric glue
    26" wood dowel
    yarn
    assorted felt pieces
    black permanent marker

Begin with an 18" x 24" piece of felt for the background. Fold one inch down on one 24" side and glue in place to make a casing. Allow to dry. Slip the dowel through the casing at the top. Tie each end of a piece of yarn to each end of the dowel for hanging.

To decorate, cut felt pieces into 1" strips and glue onto the background as a border. Cut out flower parts by freehand—stems, leaves, and flower petals. Cut the stems graduating in height. Cut out three flower pots by freehand—small, medium, and large. Glue stems, leaves, and flower petals to the flower pots with a small plant in the small pot, a medium plant in the medium pot, and a large plant in the large pot. Glue the flower pots with plants to the felt background. Place the small plant on the left and the large plant on the right with the medium plant in the middle.

Trace and cut out letters for the title, "We Are Growing." Glue the title near the top. Write "In Prayer," "In Faith," and "In Love" on the pots with a marker.

We Are One in the Lord

All the nations you have made will come and worship before you, O Lord; they will bring glory to your name. Psalm 86:9 (NIV)

All Nations Will Worship The Lord!

Materials:

Transparency Patterns:	world, international children
Background:	white paper
Border:	child pattern, tan paper
Lettering:	black
World:	light blue paper, black marker brown crayon
International Children:	white paper, assorted markers, fabric, and yarn

Directions: Cover the board. Use the pattern here to cut a border of children. Fan-fold 3 3/4" high strips of paper into 2 3/8" wide rectangles. Place the child pattern on top of the folded paper, making sure broken lines of the pattern touch folded paper edges. Cut out the child and unfold. Optional: Let students add features and costumes to represent different people around the world.

Trace and cut out the world. Outline the continents with a black marker and color the land with a brown crayon. Attach to the center of the board. Trace and cut out the international children. Add color as desired with markers, fabric, and yarn. Mount the children across the world. Add the caption.

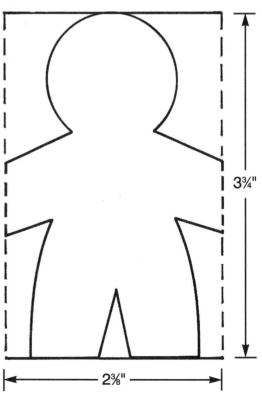

3¾"

2⅜"

People Together

Dough Recipe:
  2 cups flour
  1 cup salt
  1 cup water

Materials:
  small gingerbread man cookie cutter
  paper clip
  screen
  varnish
  1/8" wide ribbon

Make salt dough by mixing the flour and salt in a bowl. (Use whole wheat flour to make brown dough and white flour to make white dough.) Add a little water at a time to the flour and salt, mixing as you pour until the mixture forms a ball. Knead 7-10 minutes until the dough is smooth and firm. Keep the dough in a plastic bag to keep it from drying out.

Cover a flat surface with additional flour and roll the dough out to a 1/4" thickness. Use the cookie cutter to cut out three small people. Attach the people at the hands, using water to bond them. Open a paper clip and use the end to make a hole in the dough near the top of the center shape. Then use the paper clip as a tool to add features and write "PTL" on the cut-out. Let the people dry on a piece of screen for 48 hours. Varnish when dry.

When varnish is dry, thread ribbon through the hole and tie it for a necklace to wear as a reminder that all nations will worship the Lord (Psalm 86:9).

Use this idea with other verses such as Psalm 133:1, "How good and pleasant it is when brothers live together in unity!" (NIV) or Matthew 7:12, "Do to others what you would have them do to you" (NIV).

"Eye of God" (Mexico)

Materials:
  two Popsicle sticks or dowels
  assorted yarn

Look for ideas or customs from different countries or ethnic backgrounds to share in appreciation of a particular cultural heritage. This is one idea.

Crisscross two sticks, one on top of the other, to form a plus sign. Wrap yarn around them where they meet in the middle and pull tight. Weave the yarn over one stick, then under and around it. Continue weaving to the outer edge of each stick. When finished weaving, dip the end of the yarn in glue and adhere to a stick. (Variegated yarn makes a very colorful product, or you may add other colors by tying a new piece of yarn to a previous one.)

He Is Risen!

As they entered the tomb, they saw a young man dressed in a white robe sitting on the right side, and they were alarmed. "Don't be alarmed," he said. "You are looking for Jesus the Nazarene, who was crucified. He has risen! He is not here. Mark 16:5, 6 (NIV)

Materials:

Transparency Patterns:	five Jesus scenes
Background:	white paper
Border:	cross pattern, yellow paper
Lettering:	black and yellow paper, black letters
Jesus Scenes:	tan paper, permanent black marker
News Articles:	written by students in activity

Directions: Cover the board and add a cross border across the top and bottom. Use the pattern here to fan-fold 2 5/8" high strips of paper into 1 7/8" wide rectangles. Place the cross pattern on top of the folded paper, making sure broken lines of the pattern touch folded paper edges. Cut out the cross and unfold.

Cut out two star burst shapes by freehand—a large one from black paper and a slightly smaller one from yellow paper. Mount the black star burst first in the upper center of the board. Top with the yellow star burst and caption.

Trace the five Jesus scenes onto paper with a marker. Randomly post pictures on the board along with news articles written by students in the activity.

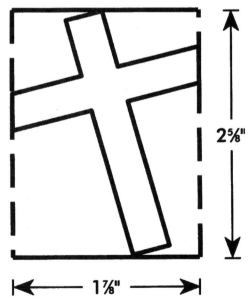

2 5/8"

1 7/8"

Pattern reprinted from *Borders Made Easy*.

On the Scene Interview

Option 1: Group students in pairs—one to conduct the interview and the other to be interviewed. Select an event leading to the resurrection of Christ and create appropriate questions to ask. Conduct a mock interview for the class. For example, the Triumphal Entry could be illustrated by conducting an interview with the disciples sent to get the colt for Jesus to ride. Use questions like these.

How did you feel when Jesus asked you to go get the colt?
Did you think the people would stop you from taking the colt?
How do you explain the people taking their cloaks off and spreading them on the road?

Option 2: Challenge students to write news articles including quotes from eye witnesses at the scene of the bulletin board pictures. Tell *who* was involved, *what* happened, *when* the event took place, *where* it took place, and *why* it happened. Post articles on the bulletin board.

Weaving

Materials:
   small safety pin
   assorted 1/4" wide ribbon
   5" square of latch hook canvas
   fabric glue
   child border pattern, page 46
   tan and light brown felt
   bias tape
   black permanent marker

Fasten a small safety pin to one end of the ribbon. Thread the pin end of the ribbon through the squares of the latch hook canvas. Alternate weaving over and under the vertical strings. Glue the other end to the back of the weaving after some is completed. Weave the entire rectangle using several colors. To finish one color, glue the end to the back weaving and start a new color.

Using the child border pattern on page 46, trace and cut out two children from the felt—one beige and one light brown. Center the two children on the weaving and glue them hand in hand. Write "He lives for you and me!" with a marker on the felt.

Cover the canvas edge with bias tape. Insert the canvas edge in the fold and glue. Glue a loop of ribbon on the back to hang the weaving.

Share the good news with a friend!

Be Ready for Every Opportunity

Then Philip ran up to the chariot and heard the man reading Isaiah the prophet. "Do you understand what you are reading" Philip asked. "How can I," he said, "unless someone explains it to me?" Acts 8:30, 31 (NIV)

Materials:

Transparency Pattern:	chariot with horses and men
Background:	light blue paper
Border:	black scalloped
Lettering:	orange
Horses:	brown paper, black marker, brown yarn, twine
Chariot and men:	white paper, assorted markers

Directions: Cover the board and attach the border around its edge.

Trace the horses separately and cut out. Add details with a marker and glue on yarn tails and manes. Rather than trace the reins, use twine as reins.

Trace and cut out the chariot and men. Add color as desired.

To mount, cut slits between the horses legs and slide in the chariot tongue. Drape reins from the horses to the man's hands. Add the caption.

Puppets

Materials:
tube socks
fabric glue
buttons
pink or red felt
yarn

Put a tube sock on your hand, pushing the toe between your thumb and other fingers for the mouth. Make marks for the eyes, nose, and tongue. Glue buttons on for the eyes and nose. Glue on a tongue made of felt and hair made of yarn. Write a play for the puppets to act out. Tell someone about Jesus.

Step On It!

Materials:
wallpaper samples
markers
index cards
die or spinner

Making the game: Cut 8" squares, triangles, and circles out of wallpaper. The number will depend upon the space available for your use. Write directions such as these on the squares.

For doing a good deed, go ahead 3 spaces.
Love in action; go ahead 2 spaces.
If you land here, take a scenic route around the temple.
For squabbling, need an even number to go ahead.

Prepare index cards by writing quotes from Bible characters about the plan of salvation (or any other subject) such as the following:

1. "I tell you the truth, no one can see the kingdom of God unless he is born again" (NIV).	John 3:3	Jesus
2. "Repent and be baptized" (NIV).	Acts 2:38	Peter
3. "Look, here is water. Why shouldn't I be baptized?" (NIV).	Acts 8:36	the Ethiopian
4. "Sirs, what must I do to be saved?" (NIV).	Acts 16:30	the jailer
5. "All have sinned and fall short of the glory of God" (NIV).	Romans 3:23	Paul

Lay the shapes on the floor to create a game board. Arrange the game board in a circle or oval; it should not have a start or a finish. Make a small loop for a detour around the temple. Alternate the pattern—circle, triangle, circle, square, circle, circle, triangle, circle, triangle, square, square, etc.

Playing the game: Take turns rolling the die or flipping the spinner. Move the number indicated. If the student lands on a square, follow the directions. If the student lands on a triangle, pick a card and read the Bible quote. If the student can identify the Bible character quoted, move ahead one space. Play the game for a set amount of time.

The Church Reaches Out

I consider my life worth nothing to me, if only I may finish the race and complete the task the Lord Jesus has given me—the task of testifying to the gospel of God's grace. Acts 20:24 (NIV)

Materials:

Transparency Patterns:	church, arm
Background:	white paper
Border:	black scalloped
Lettering:	red letters, blue marker
Church:	assorted markers or crayons
Shutters:	stiff black paper
Arms:	stiff skin-tone paper, brown marker

Directions: Cover the board and attach the border around its edge.

Trace the church directly onto the background and add details with a black marker. Color the four window scenes as desired.

Cut four window shapes from black paper for shutters. Fold each in half vertically and cut on the fold. Glue the edge of a shutter to each side of each window and fold to stand open.

Trace and cut out two arms. Outline with a marker. Fold one inch from the straight edge and attach this inch to the board, letting arms stand out from the board.

Mount letters for the roof caption. Write other words with a marker.

Reaching Out to Everyone

Materials:
international children transparency pattern or
 people of the world coloring book
white paper
assorted markers
world map
yarn
3" x 5" cards

In Matthew 28:18-20, Jesus said, "Go and make disciples of all nations, baptizing them in the name of the Father and of the Son and of the Holy Spirit, and teaching them to obey everything I have commanded you" (NIV).

Trace the international children from the transparency pattern or find a coloring book of people (American, Mexican, Japanese, Russian, Bolivian, African, Indian, German) from various places around the world. Color the pictures and cut them out. Hang a world map on the wall. Position the figures around the map. Pin a length of yarn from the figure to the country it represents.

Add cards to the display with verses that students find, showing the church reaching out to others. Here are a few examples:

Acts 10:34, 35	"God does not show favoritism but accepts men from every nation who fear him and do what is right" (NIV).
Acts 10:43	"All the prophets testify about him that everyone who believes in him receives forgiveness of sins through his name" (NIV).
Acts 13:47	"I have made you a light for the Gentiles, that you may bring salvation to the ends of the earth" (NIV).
Acts 20:35	"We must help the weak, remembering the words the Lord Jesus himself said: "It is more blessed to give then to receive'" (NIV).

Another Option: Use this activity to highlight the missions supported by your congregation. Lead students in researching information about the missions and their missionaries. Write reports and display them by the map.

Pen Pals

One way of reaching out to others is through writing. Arrange for a class to be pen pals with another Sunday school class somewhere in the country, with residents of a nursing home in your city, with a missionary family, or to shut-ins. Encourage students to write notes, letters, and poems to exchange monthly. This project could be an on-going ministry and source of encouragement to others. Students may make their own stationery or cards and include Bible verses on them.

Think About These Things

Whatever is true, whatever is noble, whatever is right, whatever is pure, whatever is lovely, whatever is admirable—if anything is excellent or praiseworthy—think about such things.
Philippians 4:8 (NIV)

Materials:

Transparency Pattern:	boy (lying down)
Background:	green and yellow paper
Border:	black scalloped
Lettering:	black letters, red paper
Boy:	white paper, assorted markers
Thought Bubble:	white paper, red, black, and blue markers

Directions: Cover the top two-thirds of the board with yellow paper and the bottom third with green paper. In addition, make grass by fringing 3" wide strips of green paper. Mount in rows across the green background. Attach the border around the edge of the board.

Trace and cut out the boy. Add color as desired. Mount the boy lying in the grass.

Cut out a large thought bubble by freehand. With markers, write in words that describe the focus of a guarded mind. Mount the large bubble with a few small bubbles above the boy's head.

Add the caption including a heart cut by freehand from red paper.

Sand Painting

Materials:

white sand

food coloring or powdered tempera paint

newspaper

tagboard

5" paper plates

Prepare colored sand by mixing food coloring or powdered tempera paint with damp sand. Spread the sand on newspaper to dry overnight. (Colored sand is available in some craft stores.)

Navajo medicine men would make intricate designs out of sand on the ground in an effort to ward off evil spirits when someone was sick. The designs were left for a number of hours and then destroyed.

In Philippians 4:4-9, Paul tells us to guard our minds and hearts with truth, nobility, righteousness, purity, loveliness, and excellence. Cut a shield shape from tagboard. Decorate it with a design to symbolize these protective virtues. Work with one color of sand at a time. Cover a small area with glue. Pinch some sand between the thumb and index finger. Sprinkle the sand over the glue. Repeat this process covering other areas where you want the same color of sand. When finished with this color, lift the tagboard up and gently shake any excess sand onto a small paper plate. Fold the paper plate to pour the excess sand in the container being used. Continue the process for each color. When the design is completed, allow it to dry for several hours.

String Art

Materials:

cross pattern, page 62

tagboard

variegated crochet thread

darning needle

Use the cross pattern on page 62 to trace a cross onto a 6" square of tagboard. Place dots and numbers on the tagboard with a pencil so marks can be erased when the project is completed. Poke a hole with a needle at each dot. Thread the needle with a single strand of crochet thread.
Tie a knot at the end of the thread. Starting in the back of the tagboard, bring the needle to the front of the board through hole #1. Push the needle down through #29 to take the needle back behind the tagboard. Follow the guide below. The first number comes up from behind the tagboard; the second number indicates the needle going from the front of the tagboard, down through the hole, and to the back (i.e., 1/29).

First: 1/29, 2/30, 3/31, 4/32, 5/33.
Second: 5/53, 6/54, 7/55, 8/56, 9/1.
Third: 16/9, 17/10, 18/11, 19/12, 20/13.
Fourth: 20/33, 21/34, 22/35, 23/36, 24/37, 25/38, 26/39, 27/40, 28/41, 29/42.
Fifth: 49/42, 50/43, 51/44, 52/45, 53/46.
Sixth: 9/42, 53/20.

Tape the end of the thread to the back. Draw a heart around the cross with a marker. Write "Guard your heart" (Philippians 4:4-9) at the bottom of the board.

Jesus First in All Things

Seek first his kingdom and his righteousness. Matthew 6:33 (NIV)

Materials:

Transparency Pattern:	Jesus 1st
Background:	red
Border:	white paper
	red, purple, green markers
Lettering:	yellow
Jesus 1st:	yellow paper, red and purple markers

Directions: Cover the board. Cut border paper into 3" x 5" strips. Write "#1" on strips in alternating marker colors and mount.

Trace and cut out Jesus 1st. Color "J-E-S-U-S" red and outline with a purple marker. Attach to the right side of the board with the caption on the left.

Heaven's Treasure

Materials:
   small box
   tempera paint
   glitter
   yellow paper

In Mark 10:17-22, Jesus told a man that if he would keep the commandments and sell his possessions and give them to the poor, then he would have treasures in heaven. James 1:22 tells us to be doers of the Word.

Make a treasure chest by painting a box and trimming it with glitter. Write "Heaven's Treasures" on the side of the chest. Cut "coins" or circles out of yellow paper. Have students write a good deed they did that week on each coin. Put their coins in the treasure chest. Challenge students to do good deeds in the upcoming week. Make a chart of suggestions and encourage students to add their ideas to the list. Include: volunteer to help at home, school , or church; be a friend to someone who is lonely; pick up litter in the neighborhood; write a letter to a relative or a shut-in; read the Bible to someone who can't read.

His Light Shines

Materials:
   9" aluminum pie plate
   cross pattern, page 19 (optional)
   cardboard
   Styrofoam
   large nail
   votive candle

Fold an aluminum pie plate in half. Then unfold. Make a cardboard pattern of the cross on page 19 or the number one with J-E-S-U-S written vertically inside (similar to the bulletin board). Size to fit in one half of the pie plate with the fold being the base line.

Place the open pie plate, bottom down, onto Styrofoam. Place the cross or number one pattern inside the pie plate. Position the bottom of the pattern near the fold line. Use a nail to punch holes about every 1/4" around the pattern. Do this on the Styrofoam which will serve as a buffer and protect the surface on which you are working. Remove the pattern.

Fold the pie plate so that the punched side is standing up and the plain side is flat on the table, making a 90° angle. Place a candle on the unpunched side.

Burn the candle to observe the punched design. The candle holder will be a reminder to students to put Jesus first and to let his light shine through them. *Caution students* to always have an adult's permission before burning the candle.

God Takes Care of Us

Then Moses raised his arm and struck the rock twice with his staff.
Water gushed out, and the community and their livestock drank. Numbers 20:11 (NIV)

Materials:

Transparency Pattern:	Moses
Background:	green paper
Border:	yellow scalloped
Lettering:	yellow
Rocks:	gray paper, gray marker
Water:	blue paper, clear cellophane
Moses:	white paper, assorted markers and fabric, twine, stick

Directions: Cover the board. Cut out several large rocks by freehand and mount to the right side of the board. Use a marker to add pebbles to the ground. Cut out water by freehand to flow from the rocks. Cover the paper with clear cellophane for a "wet" look and mount. Attach the border around the edge of the board.

Trace and cut out Moses. Add color as desired with markers and fabric. Glue on twine for his belt and headpiece tie. Instead of tracing the stick, add a real stick. Mount Moses to the left side of the board.

Add the caption.

God Provides

Materials:

rocks cut out of gray paper   markers

As the Israelites wandered throughout the wilderness, God provided for their every need. Today, he also provides for our every need. To foster an awareness of how God is working in their own lives, direct students to think about the needs they have. Think about the ways in which those needs are met.

Brainstorm to make a list of needs that God has provided. Write the needs on rocks and add them to the bulletin board.

Challenge

Prepare slips of paper naming ways students may help others. Put them in a jar.

The Israelites were complaining about being thirsty. God told Moses to speak to the rocks, and he gave them clear, fresh, thirst-quenching water to drink. Ask students if they are willing to let God use them to met the needs of others? Let students draw jobs out of the jar and challenge them to do their tasks in the coming week. Report next time on particular blessings or needs that have been met.

Thirst Quencher

Materials:

manila folders	yarn
assorted markers	Bible
paper fasteners	concordance

Let students find Scriptures where God has met the needs of people in a special way, and make a folder game. Open the folder. List the events on one side of the folder. List the Bible references on the other side. Put a paper fastener beside each event and each reference. Tie a length of yarn (long enough to reach the other side of the folder) around each paper fastener next to an event.

Challenge a classmate to match the event and the Bible reference by wrapping yarn around the paper fasteners. For example:

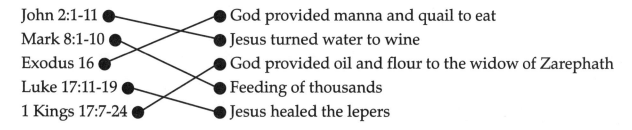

This can be an exercise in memory work, locating Scriptures, or using a concordance.

Jesus Hears Our Prayers

Therefore I tell you, whatever you ask for in prayer, believe that you have received it, and it will be yours. Mark 11:24 (NIV)

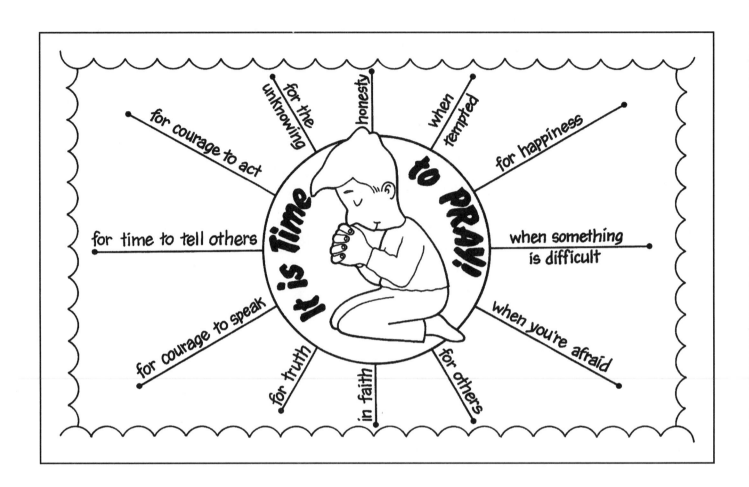

Materials:

Transparency Pattern:	praying boy
Background:	blue paper
Border:	red scalloped
Lettering:	black letters, black marker
Center Circle:	red paper
Lines:	red yarn
Praying Boy:	white paper, assorted markers

Directions: Cover the board and attach the border around its edge. Cut a large paper circle and mount in the center of the board. Stretch twelve yarn lines from the circle to the border and attach.

Trace and cut out the praying boy. Add color as desired. Mount the boy in the center circle.

Mount the caption around the boy in the circle. Attach with a straight pin at the top and bottom of each letter. Pull the letters forward so they stand out from the board.

Write reasons and times to pray on the yarn lines with a marker.

Prayer Time

Materials:
blank calendar
Bibles

With the class, make a prayer and activity calendar. Include Bible verses when appropriate. Choose activities and suggestions as a group and write them on the calendar. For example, one week may look like this:

Sunday	Read Job 33:4. Take a big breath. Then let it out. Praise God for the gift of life!
Monday	Read Matthew 6:9-13. Pray the model prayer with your family.
Tuesday	Read Matthew 2:13-15. Thank God for the ways he keeps your family safe.
Wednesday	Read Matthew 2:11. Give a gift to Jesus. Praise God for Jesus.
Thursday	Complete this prayer. "God, thank you for _____."
Friday	Pray for the leaders of your youth group.
Saturday	Pray for the missionaries your church supports.

Another Option: Write the names of people to pray for on each square of the calendar. These could be general or specific such as family, friends, grandparents, youth group, teachers, preacher, cousins, school, and President.

Prayer Journal

Materials:
8 1/2" x 11" typing paper
9" x 12" colored paper
stapler
assorted markers and crayons

Make a prayer journal by folding typing paper in half. Fold a sheet of 9" x 12" colored paper in half for the cover. Put the typing paper inside of the cover and staple the journal at the fold. Design a cover. Write headings at the top of the inside pages for general topics such as praises, requests, confessions, family, friends, school, church, and nation.

Encourage students to keep a prayer journal each day by writing the date of specific praises and requests they make during their daily prayer time. Leave space to note the date of answered prayer. This activity not only makes students aware of the need for prayer but also helps them to see how God answers their prayers.

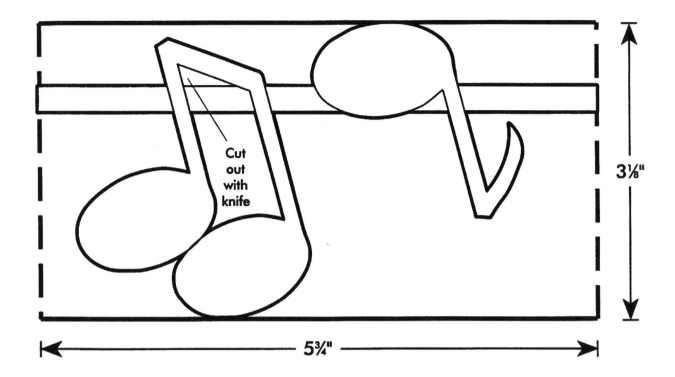

Cut out with knife

3⅛"

5¾"

Pattern reprinted from *Borders Made Easy*.

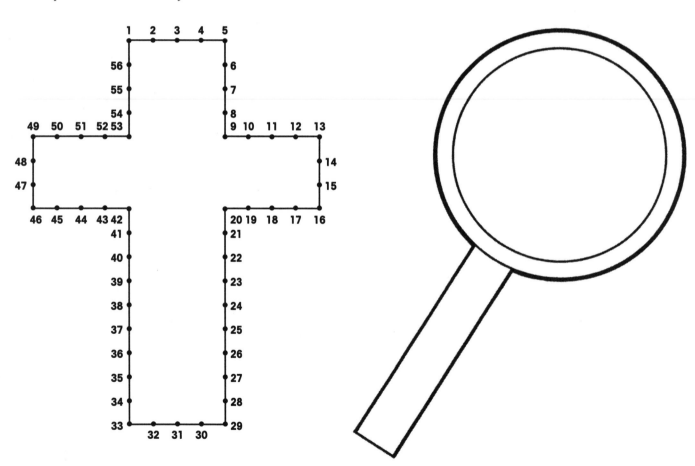